# A Child's Book of Virtues

### BY KAY McSPADDEN

*The ogres ran from the tower and saw Little Peachling with his animal companions standing fiercely at his side, ready for battle.*

STAMPLEY

STAMPLEY

Also by Kay McSpadden
*Notes from a Classroom: Reflections on Teaching*

Stampley offers special discounts on titles purchased in quantity
for gifts, premiums, fundraisers and educational use.
For more information, write to us at:

C.D. Stampley Enterprises
Attention: Special Sales
P.O. Box 33172, Charlotte, NC 28233 USA
or email sales@stampley.com.

Published exclusively by
C.D. Stampley Enterprises, Inc.
in association with Creations for Children International

**Library of Congress Cataloging-in-Publication Data**

McSpadden, Kay, 1956-
A child's book of virtues / by Kay McSpadden.
    p. cm.
ISBN 978-1-58087-156-3
1. Virtues--Juvenile literature.  I. Title.

BJ1521.M37 2010
179'.9--dc22

                                                2010006602

Printed in China — 2010
www.stampley.com

# CONTENTS

# INTRODUCTION

**WHY WE LIKE STORIES**

Everyone loves a good story. All over the world, from the beginning of history until today, people have come together to share stories in the evenings or when their work was done.

People love stories for different reasons. Some stories make us laugh. Others awaken our sense of danger or suspense, or our wonder at faraway places. But the very best stories, the ones we read over and over again, are ones that teach us about virtue.

The word "virtue" comes from the Latin word for "strength" — and in fact virtues are the character traits that strengthen us to lead good and happy lives. In this book you will read about fourteen virtues, including perseverance, hope, compassion and loyalty. These stories are a great way to learn about what makes a virtuous life.

Some stories introduce us to characters who act virtuously even when it's difficult. These characters can become our heroes and role models. Other stories show us characters who reject or ignore virtue — providing examples of poor choices to avoid.

**WHERE STORIES COME FROM**

Sometimes stories are very old, and sometimes they are modern. Some stories about virtues are made up, or fiction, and others are true stories that happened to real people.

One of the oldest stories we know of is about the Greek hero Odysseus (o-DISS-eeus). Odysseus's trip home from the Trojan War is a tale of many fantastic adventures, one of which is retold in this book. In my high school classroom where I teach English, my 12th graders begin the school year reading about Odysseus and his journey. Even students ready to graduate from high school love his story!

This book also includes other stories from classic literature, including the tale of poor Don Quixote who read so much about medieval knights he thought he could become a character in one of his books! You can also read about Huck Finn, another character loved by children and adults alike, and see what he decides to do when he has to make a very hard choice between helping his friend Jim or helping himself. Another character who is faced with a difficult decision is Jean Valjean from the book *Les Misérables.* Jean fails to act virtuously when he chooses to steal. But his failure leads to a very surprising outcome!

Tales and fables are another kind of fictional story included in this book. Tales and fables are stories created especially to teach children about virtue. "Little Peachling," for example, is a story about being a generous friend and a good son. "The Amazing Dream" is a story from a faraway country about a man who dares to follow his dream — and what happens when he does.

Finally, this book also includes true stories about people whose lives have much to teach us. It might seem like it would be sad to learn about the life of a young blind, deaf girl, but the story of Helen Keller and how her teacher Annie Sullivan taught her about language is an inspiration to everyone who reads it. Another historical character who teaches us about virtue is Brother Martin, a friar from Peru who helps a beggar one night.

### WE NEVER STOP LEARNING FROM STORIES

The stories in *A Child's Book of Virtues* have been selected and told with young people in mind. But no one is ever too old to enjoy a good story, especially one that teaches us how to live. Even my high school students love stories about virtue. Their favorite stories are ones with characters like themselves who are asked to make difficult choices — to show compassion to the poor or outcasts, to persevere in following their dreams, to pick themselves up and learn from their mistakes.

In this book you will read stories about many different virtues, and you will read stories that are both real and fictional. Like all good stories, they are fun and entertaining. But best of all, each story offers a special glimpse of what it means to live virtuously — the great adventure we all must undertake.

— Kay McSpadden

# LITTLE PEACHLING

In Japan there lived a woodcutter and his wife whose only sorrow was they never had any children. One day the wife was washing clothes in the river when she saw a large peach floating by. "I'll take this home for my husband," she thought, but just then the peach split open and a tiny baby crawled out.

The woodcutter and his wife were happy to have a child of their own. They named him Little Peachling. Little Peachling grew big and strong. His parents loved him so much they often went without dinner so he could have more to eat.

As he grew older, Little Peachling began to understand that his parents lived a hard life without many comforts. One day he asked his parents to make him some dumplings. "I am going to the ogres' castle to take back their plunder," he told his parents. Though they were afraid for him, they did as he asked and gave him some dumplings for the journey.

No sooner had Little Peachling started than he saw a monkey swinging from a tree. "Little Peachling," the

monkey called, "if you give me a dumpling, I will share your journey." Little Peachling was glad for the company so he gave the monkey a dumpling.

Soon the two of them saw a peacock overhead. "Little Peachling," she called, "if you will give me a dumpling, I will share your journey." Little Peachling gave the peacock a dumpling, and the three of them headed further into the woods.

Soon they saw a dog who also asked for a dumpling. "I'm going to the ogres' castle to get the treasure they've plundered," Little Peachling told the monkey, peacock and dog. "Are you sure you want to share my journey now?" But the three animal friends were happy to go with Little Peachling.

When they arrived at the ogres' castle, the monkey climbed over the wall and opened the gate to let Little Peachling in. Then the peacock flew to the topmost tower of the castle and looked in. "I saw only three ogres," she said, and the dog began to bark.

The ogres ran from the tower and saw Little Peachling with his animal companions standing fiercely at his side, ready for battle. "Take what you want and don't hurt us!" they cried, and Little Peachling loaded his backpack with gold and jewels.

When he arrived home that night, Little Peachling gave the treasure to his parents, and they all lived in comfort for the rest of their lives.

*The ogres ran from the tower and saw Little Peachling with his animal companions standing fiercely at his side, ready for battle. "Take what you want and don't hurt us!" they cried, and Little Peachling loaded his backpack with gold and jewels.*

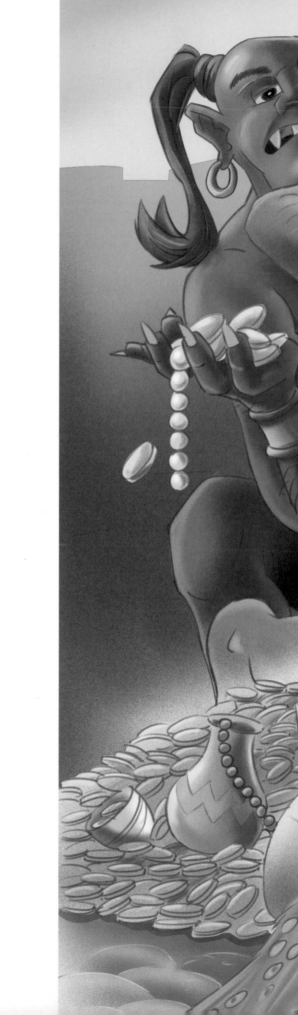

# THE AMAZING DREAM

Once there was a bookseller in Baghdad who lived in a small house with a tiny garden full of flowers. One night after a long day spent pulling his heavy cart of books, the bookseller dreamed he was in Cairo, Egypt, walking along the sunlit streets. In his dream he found a policeman who handed him a pile of gold coins.

The dream was so real that when the bookseller woke he decided to journey to Cairo to find the generous policeman.

He arrived in Cairo and spent three days walking the streets. The sun was hot and the hours long, but the bookseller didn't get discouraged. Finally as the sun was setting on the third day he saw a familiar-looking policeman. The bookseller rushed up to him and told him his amazing dream.

"You have wasted your time," the policeman scoffed. "Dreams aren't real. Just last night I dreamed I dug up a pile of gold coins in a tiny flower garden in Baghdad, but I knew better than to be hopeful."

The bookseller thanked the policeman and journeyed home with a smile. When he arrived in Baghdad he dug up the gold coins in his own garden.

*Finally as the sun was setting on the third day he saw a familiar-looking policeman. The bookseller rushed up to him and told him his amazing dream.*

# NIKKI TIKKI TUMBO

A long time ago in a faraway land, first-born sons were considered very important and were given very long names. All other children had short names.

One family had two boys, Nikki Tikki Tumbo No Sar Rumbo Ali Bali Bushkie Bolli Wolli Bee Chi and his little brother Yu. Often their mother would warn them, "Do not play near the well!" But like little boys everywhere, sometimes they did not listen.

One day the brothers were playing near the well and Yu fell in!

Nikki Tikki Tumbo No Sar Rumbo Ali Bali Bushkie Bolli Wolli Bee Chi ran as fast as he could back to his house.

"Mother!" he cried. "Yu has fallen into the well!" His mother was busy stirring a pot of noodles but she dropped her spoon and yelled, "Hurry! Go get the old gardener to take his ladder to the well!"

So Nikki Tikki Tumbo No Sar Rumbo Ali Bali Bushkie Bolli Wolli Bee Chi ran as fast as he could to the old gardener.

"Old gardener!" he cried. "Please bring your ladder and help my brother Yu who has fallen into the well!"

The gardener was very old indeed, and he moved slowly to the shed where he kept his ladder. Then he followed Nikki Tikki Tumbo No Sar Rumbo Ali Bali Bushkie Bolli Wolli Bee Chi back to the well. He put the ladder in and climbed down. There he found Yu, cold and tired from swimming.

"Let that be a lesson to you both!" the boys' mother said that night as she sent them to bed without any noodles.

But soon enough the brothers were once again playing near the well, and one day Nikki Tikki

Tumbo No Sar Rumbo Ali Bali Bushkie Bolli Wolli Bee Chi fell in!

Poor Yu ran as fast as his short legs would take him back home.

"Mother!" he cried. "Nikki Tikki Tumbo No Sar Rumbo Ali Bali Bushkie Bolli Wolli Bee Chi has fallen into the well!"

Yu's mother was busy feeding the chickens and couldn't hear over their clucking. "Speak up!" she shouted, so Yu tried again.

"Nikki Tikki Tumbo No Sar Rumbo Ali Bali Bushkie Bolli Wolli Bee Chi has fallen into the well!"

This time Yu's mother heard him.

"Go get the old gardener to take his ladder to the well!" So Yu ran as fast as his little legs would take him to the old gardener.

"Old gardener!" Yu shouted. "Please bring your ladder! Nikki Tikki Tumbo No Sar Rumbo Ali Bali Bushkie Bolli Wolli Bee Chi has fallen into the well!"

The old gardener was just waking from a nap and he said, "Who's calling me?" Yu tried again. "Please bring your ladder! Nikki Tikki Tumbo No Sar Rumbo Ali Bali Bushkie Bolli Wolli Bee Chi has fallen into the well!"

The old gardener cupped his hand behind his ear and said, "Speak up! My ears are old!"

Poor Yu was panting heavily from running and from having to say that great long name so many times. But he knew his brother needed help. He took a deep breath, then said as loud as he could:

"Nikki Tikki Tumbo No Sar Rumbo Ali Bali Buskie Bolli Wolli Bee Chi is in the well!"

Finally the gardener understood. He grabbed his ladder and followed Yu to the well. Nikki Tikki Tumbo No Sar Rumbo Ali Bali Bushkie Bolli Wolli Bee Chi had been in the water so long he was shivering with cold. The old gardener climbed down the ladder and pulled him from the well.

Once back on dry ground, Nikki Tikki Tumbo No Sar Rumbo Ali Bali Bushkie Bolli Wolli Bee Chi sputtered, caught his breath and promised he would never play near the well again. Because he was in the well so long he caught a cold and was sick in bed for three days — but Yu had brought help just in time!

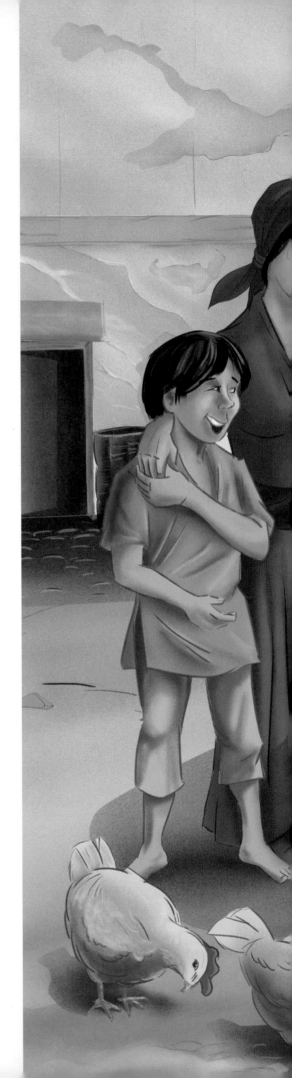

*Once back on dry ground, Nikki Tikki Tumbo No Sar Rumbo Ali Bali Bushkie Bolli Wolli Bee Chi sputtered, caught his breath and promised he would never play near the well again.*

# THE BANYAN DEER

In the forests of India there once lived a beautiful golden deer with silver antlers.

He was called the Banyan Deer and he was king of a large herd. In the same forest lived another herd, ruled by a king called the Monkey Deer. Both the Monkey Deer and the Banyan Deer took their responsibilities as kings very seriously.

The forest was a lovely place with large trees and running streams. If it hadn't been for the sultan, the deer would have been happy indeed.

The sultan was a rich man who loved to hunt deer. Each day he and his servants would travel into the forest and shoot their arrows. The only deer the sultan didn't try to kill were the Banyan Deer and the Monkey Deer.

"Leave those deer alone," he warned his servants. "With their golden fur and their silver antlers, they are too beautiful to kill."

So the servants did not try to kill the Banyan Deer and the Monkey Deer, but they killed and hurt many of the others.

Finally the Banyan Deer said to the Monkey Deer, "The hunters are killing and wounding too many of us. Why don't we take turns sending one deer each day to the hunters? That way the hunters will stay out of the forest and fewer deer will be lost."

The Monkey Deer agreed, and from then on one deer would leave the forest each day and go to the hunters before they could bother anyone else.

One day a mother deer came to the Monkey Deer and said, "It is my turn to go to the hunters, but I have a young fawn. Let me stay with him until he gets older and then I will take my turn."

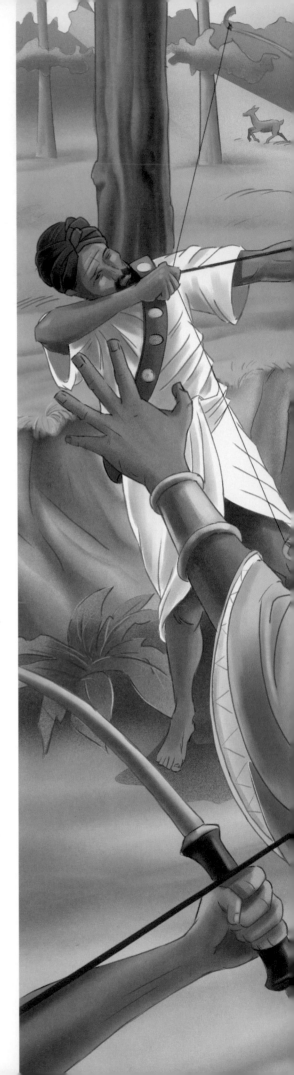

The Monkey Deer replied, "If it is your turn, you must go."

The mother deer then went to the Banyan Deer and asked what she could do.

"Go home and take care of your fawn," he said.

The next day when the hunters approached the forest, the Banyan Deer walked out and offered himself to them. The sultan was surprised.

"Why are you offering to die?" he asked. "Don't you know that I have told my hunters to spare your life?"

The Banyan Deer told the sultan about the mother deer.

"I could not ask anyone else to take her place," the Banyan Deer said, "so I have come instead."

"You are a true leader," the sultan replied, "and from this day forward I will never hunt you nor your deer again."

*The next day when the hunters approached the forest, the Banyan Deer walked out and offered himself to them. The sultan was surprised. "Why are you offering to die?" he asked.*

# RAINBOW CROW

The first time snow came to the earth the animals were pleased. But when the snow did not stop the animals began to suffer from the cold.

"We must send a message to The Creator Who Creates By Thinking What Will Be," said Wise Owl. "We must ask him to think the world warm again."

The animals began to debate who among them should travel to The Creator. Wise Owl couldn't see well in daylight. Coyote was a trickster and could not be trusted.

Turtle offered but he was too slow. Finally Rainbow Crow volunteered. He was the most beautiful bird in the land, with red, green and blue feathers and a lovely singing voice.

For three days and three nights Rainbow Crow flew, passing the moon, the sun and the stars. At last he came to The Creator. He began to sing a beautiful song to get The Creator's attention.

"Come here, Rainbow Crow," The Creator said. "Let me reward you for your beautiful song. What can I do for you?"

Rainbow Crow asked The Creator to take away the snow.

"I can't un-think snow," The Creator said, "but I can give you something to keep the animals warm."

With that The Creator took a large stick, stuck it into the sun until it burst into flame, and handed the burning stick to Rainbow Crow.

Rainbow Crow flew back to earth as fast as he could. As he flew past the stars and the sun, soot from the fire turned his feathers black. As he passed the moon, the smoke from the fire caught in his throat, changing his beautiful singing voice into a hoarse caw.

The animals were delighted with the fire that Rainbow Crow brought. Once again they were warm and safe. However, Rainbow Crow was quite upset about what had happened to him.

Then one day he saw The Creator walking towards him.

"Don't be sad," The Creator said. "Your sacrifice has made the lives of many much better. And as for you, when people come to the earth you will not be hunted because your flesh tastes of smoke. No one will want your black feathers, nor will people put you in a cage to sing for them. You will always be a free bird."

Then The Creator said, "When you look at your feathers in the sunlight you will see the rainbow and remember your sacrifice."

And Rainbow Crow's heart was glad.

# PRINCE CHERRY

Once there was a king who was so good and wise that a fairy named Candide offered him any gift he should desire.

"Make my son, Prince Cherry, a good man," the king said, but Candide shook her head.

"Prince Cherry must make himself a good man," said Candide. "However, I will be his friend, always giving him the advice he needs."

The king was satisfied. Years later, he remembered Candide's promise on his deathbed and he died in peace.

At first Prince Cherry was as good and kind as his father. Slowly, however, he became used to the special treatment he received as king. He grew irritable and impatient with his servants and friends. When he kicked his pet dog, Prince Cherry was startled to hear a voice in his ear.

"I am the fairy Candide," said the voice. "You must learn to be a good man."

Candide's warning prompted Prince Cherry to behave better for a time. But he soon fell back into treating everyone around him very badly.

One day as he rode through his kingdom, Prince Cherry saw a beautiful girl named Zelia. She was so lovely and sweet-natured that Prince Cherry knelt down in front of her and asked her to marry him.

"I'm sorry, Prince Cherry," Zelia said, "but I will only marry someone truly good and kind."

Prince Cherry was furious. He ordered his servants to lock Zelia in the palace dungeon. Just then Prince Cherry heard a voice in his ear. "You have become more horrible than the worst beast on earth," it said. And with that, Prince Cherry was transformed into a monster! He had a bull's head, a lion's mane, a wolf's paws and a snake's tail. He was horrified at the

change in his appearance and rushed to hide himself in the woods.

Before long Prince Cherry was captured by hunters and put on display at the zoo. He was humiliated and ashamed, but there was nothing he could do.

Then one day a lion escaped from its cage and attacked the zoo keeper. Although the zoo keeper had not been kind to Prince Cherry, the prince forced the lion back into its cage.

A voice in his ear said, "No good deed goes unnoticed," and suddenly Prince Cherry was transformed from a terrible beast into a little dog. The zoo keeper picked him up and took him home to be a pet for his children.

Prince Cherry was ashamed to live as a dog, but he resolved to make the lives of the children happy by being the best pet possible.

One day when he was eating the single bread crust that was his daily meal, he saw a hungry old beggar woman walking by. Carefully Prince Cherry carried the crust of bread to the old woman and dropped it at her feet.

A voice in his ear said, "No good deed goes unnoticed," and Prince Cherry was transformed once again, this time into a white dove. He flew far and wide across the land looking for Zelia.

"Perhaps I can let her know how sorry I am," he thought, but several years went by before he finally saw her sitting at a window. Prince Cherry landed on her shoulder and Zelia said, "Ah, pretty dove, you have come to cheer me up. If you stay here with me, I will love you forever."

Suddenly Prince Cherry felt himself changing

*Prince Cherry was transformed into a monster! He had a bull's head, a lion's mane, a wolf's paws and a snake's tail.*

back into the shape of a man.

With a flash of light, the fairy Candide appeared, and Prince Cherry recognized her voice as she said, "You have proven yourself worthy of love at last. With the lessons you have learned and with the love of Zelia, go and be the good king that your father hoped you could be."

*A voice in his ear said, "No good deed goes unnoticed," and Prince Cherry was transformed once again, this time into a white dove. He flew far and wide across the land looking for Zelia.*

# ROLAND AND OLIVER

With a loud clang, Oliver's sword broke. He couldn't believe it! Now he stood defenseless against Roland, the strongest warrior in France.

The two young men had been fighting for hours. Roland was the nephew of King Charlemagne, and Oliver was the grandson of Count Gerard. Months earlier King Charlemagne and Count Gerard had gotten into a terrible argument. Their angry words had turned into angry actions that were hurting all of France.

At first Count Gerard simply retreated behind his castle walls and barred the gates.

He and his soldiers had plenty of food and water, and they vowed not to come out until King Charlemagne apologized.

King Charlemagne's men camped out around Count Gerard's castle and shot arrows over the towers. They cut down the trees in the orchards and trampled the fields. Soon the crops were destroyed and the peasants living nearby were terrified.

The soldiers on both sides appealed to their leaders to give up their argument, but both King Charlemagne and Count Gerard were stubborn. Finally one of their advisors had a plan: Choose one fighter to represent each side and let them fight each other. The rest of the soldiers could go back to defending their country and the peasants could stop being afraid and could start farming again.

On the designated day, Roland and Oliver met on an island in the middle of the Rhone River and began their fight. Then Oliver's sword broke. He was sure Roland would kill him and King Charlemagne could claim victory.

But Roland put down his own sword instead.

34

"I won't fight an unarmed man," he said, and he called for his assistant to bring a new sword for Oliver.

Once again the men began fighting. This time Roland's shield crumpled when Oliver hit it hard.

"I won't fight a man without a shield," Oliver said, and both men threw their shields and swords down and began fighting hand-to-hand without weapons.

Suddenly in their wrestling, both Oliver and Roland grabbed each other's helmets and tugged. They both fell backwards, their helmets in their opponent's hands.

When Roland looked at Oliver, Oliver looked back. Then they slowly rose and reached out their hands to shake.

King Charlemagne and Count Gerard were amazed.

"If these two worthy soldiers can respect each other, then we should be able to do the same," King Charlemagne said, and Count Gerard agreed. They apologized to each other for their long feud and resolved to work together for the good of France.

*When Roland looked at Oliver, Oliver looked back. Then they slowly rose and reached out their hands to shake.*

# BROTHER MARTIN AND THE BEGGAR

Martin de Porres had a special love for the poor. As the son of a former slave in Lima, Peru, Martin knew what it was to be poor and abandoned. His experiences as a child helped give Martin a special compassion for others.

When he became a teenager Martin joined a friary as a humble worker. He was often seen sweeping, cleaning and doing other helpful tasks. Later Martin became a friar himself. Martin always kept an eye out for the hungry and poor, sharing with them what little he had.

Once a homeless man covered with sores came to the friary begging. Martin was so moved with pity he gave up his own bed to the man. One of his fellow friars was upset and scolded Martin for doing too much. The beggar in Martin's bed was filthy!

Martin replied, "Being compassionate is more important than being clean. After all, with a little bit of soap I can clean my bed. But if I had not offered kindness to this poor man, I would have put a stain on my soul that a flood of tears could not wash away."

For the rest of his life Martin continued to show great compassion for the poor people of Peru.

*Once a homeless man covered with sores came to the friary begging. Martin was so moved with pity he gave up his own bed to the man.*

# HELEN LEARNS ABOUT LANGUAGE

Close your eyes and cover your ears. Imagine what your life would be like if you could not see or hear. That's what life was like for Helen Keller.

Helen was not yet two years old when an illness left her blind and deaf. Although Helen had known a few words, she quickly forgot them. Instead, she learned to make motions to show what she wanted. For example, she pretended to rock a baby when she wanted to play with her doll.

Without real words, however, Helen wasn't able to communicate very much. She began to throw frequent tantrums. In despair, her mother and father took her to many doctors. Finally they found Annie Sullivan, a young teacher who had also once had trouble with her vision.

Helen's mother immediately had faith that Annie could help Helen. She watched as Annie held Helen's hand and spelled out letters in her palm.

Annie spelled D-O-L-L in sign language. Then she put a doll in Helen's hand. Still, Helen did not seem to understand that Annie's finger motions and the doll meant the same thing.

For weeks Annie spelled words for Helen, but Helen seemed locked inside her dark, silent world. If only Annie could find a way to make Helen under- stand the idea of words! Annie was sure that words would open up Helen's world.

One day Helen was in a cranky mood and dumped a pitcher of water at dinner.

Helen's mother and father didn't know how to handle the tantrum. But Annie insisted Helen refill the pitcher at the pump in the front yard. She took Helen to the pump and spelled P-U-M-P into her hand. Helen ignored her and tried to get away.

40

Annie held Helen's hand tightly and started pumping the water. As it rushed over their hands, Annie spelled W-A-T-E-R. Suddenly Helen stopped squirming. An odd expression came over her face. Annie spelled W-A-T-E-R into Helen's palm again.

Slowly Helen spelled the word back into Annie's palm. Then she did something that she hadn't done in four years — she tried to speak!

Before her illness, one of the words that Helen had known was "water." Now she remembered the word and tried to say it, but she said "wa-wa," the way a baby would.

That didn't matter to Annie. What mattered was that Helen finally understood the idea of words and language. No longer would she have to hope that someone would understand what she needed and wanted. With language, Helen could express her deepest thoughts and desires. With language, her mind was finally free.

*An odd expression came over Helen's face as Annie spelled W-A-T-E-R into Helen's palm. Slowly Helen spelled the word back into Annie's palm. Then she did something that she hadn't done in four years — she tried to speak!*

# FREDERICK LEARNS TO READ

Frederick Douglass grew up to be a famous speaker and writer, but he almost didn't learn to read!

Frederick was born a slave in Maryland in 1817. When he was eight years old, he was sent to live with the Aulds, a white family with a son Frederick's age. Mrs. Auld taught both boys the alphabet.

Because teaching slaves to read was against the law, Mrs. Auld was forced to stop Frederick's lessons. Now instead of encouraging him, Mrs. Auld kept books away from him. This made Frederick want to read even more. Somehow he knew that reading was the key to becoming educated.

Although the Aulds would not let Frederick learn to read, they did feed him well, and most afternoons he would put bread in his pockets and wait outside the school that many of the local boys attended.

Their families were poor and the boys were hungry, so Frederick made a deal with them. If they would teach him to read, he would give them food.

Just as slave owners feared, reading made Frederick powerful. He read newspaper stories about abolitionists who wanted to get rid of slavery, and this gave him hope that one day he would be free.

*Frederick made a deal with them. If they would teach him to read, he would give them food.*

# ODYSSEUS AND THE CYCLOPS

Of all the heroes in Greek mythology, Odysseus was by far the smartest. He created the Trojan Horse, a trick which helped the Greeks win the Trojan War.

Even though he was smart, Odysseus had trouble getting back home after the war. He and his crew of sailors ran into one misadventure after another. One of the scariest was the time they met the Cyclops.

The Cyclops was a giant who had only one large eye in the middle of his forehead. He and his brothers lived in caves and raised sheep that they took to the meadows every day to graze.

One day Odysseus and his men pulled their boat up to the beach near the Cyclops' cave. They were tired and hungry as they went to the cave entrance.

"Who's there?" the Cyclops called.

When Odysseus saw the hideous monster, he was alarmed, so he said, "My name is No Man. My crew and I need some food and drink."

"I have plenty!" the Cyclops said, but as soon as the sailors went into the cave, he grabbed two of them and swallowed them whole! Then he rolled a large boulder in front of the cave entrance so that no one could leave.

The next morning the Cyclops ate two more of Odysseus's men before taking his sheep outside to the meadow. When the last sheep left the cave, the Cyclops sealed the boulder back in place.

All day Odysseus sharpened a stick and waited for the Cyclops to return. Soon enough he heard the boulder rolling back. As soon as his sheep were inside, the Cyclops sealed the cave entrance back up. Odysseus jumped forward and with a quick jab poked the Cyclops in the eye. The terrible monster began screaming loudly.

47

Almost at once his brothers came running to the cave.

"Why are you yelling?" they asked from outside the entrance. "No Man is hurting me!" the Cyclops said.

"Then stop bothering us," the brothers said, and they left.

The next morning after the Cyclops opened the cave, he kept his hands outstretched to make sure the sailors did not try to escape when the sheep left for the meadow. Odysseus had told his men to hold onto the wool bellies of the sheep and hang upside down. That way the Cyclops would feel the backs of the sheep and not realize that the men were escaping.

The plan worked perfectly, and Odysseus and his men made it safely out of the cave and down to their boat on the beach. Once more Odysseus was able to use his wits to save the day!

*Odysseus had told his men to hold onto the wool bellies of the sheep and hang upside down. That way the Cyclops would feel the backs of the sheep and not realize that the men were escaping.*

# DON QUIXOTE AND THE GIANTS

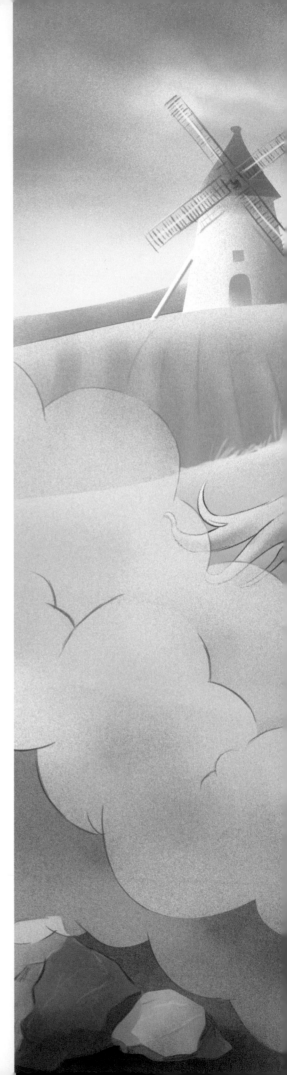

Once in Spain there lived a frail old man named Don Quixote. He loved to read books about knights and their adventures from long ago. Don Quixote read so many books he forgot he was frail and old and decided he would search for adventure as a knight too!

His family reminded him that the Middle Ages were over and knights did not ride off on adventures anymore.

But Don Quixote didn't care. First he donned an old rusty suit of armor that had been passed down in his family. Then he gave his poor, skinny, bowlegged horse a fancy name, Rocinante, which means The Horse That Used to Be Skinny and Bowlegged. He asked an innkeeper to dub him a knight. Finally he asked Sancho Panza, a farmer, to serve as his squire.

None of these things made Don Quixote a real knight, but he wasn't thinking very clearly. He wanted to ride forth into the world and do the kinds of good deeds that knights had done in his books.

Early one morning Don Quixote and Sancho Panza left their village and rode uphill and down looking for someone to help. Suddenly in the distance Don Quixote spotted something of interest.

"Look, Sancho!" he cried. "I see three evil giants waving their arms at me! The world will be a better place when I get rid of them!"

Sancho looked where Don Quixote was pointing. "Where are the giants?" Sancho asked. "All I see are three windmills with their sails blowing in the wind."

"You are mistaken," Don Quixote told Sancho. "I have read many books about knights, so I know what giants look like. I'm going to fight them!"

Sancho tried once more to convince Don Quixote of the truth.

"I haven't read any books," Sancho said, "but I can see that those are windmills for grinding grain."

"Poor Sancho!" Don Quixote laughed, and he rode off as fast as poor old Rocinante could carry him. He aimed his lance right at the sail of the windmill.

Just then a puff of wind turned the sail and Don Quixote was knocked off his horse.

Sancho rushed up but Don Quixote was unhurt. "See," Sancho said. "I told you those were windmills."

Don Quixote stood up and dusted himself off. "They might be windmills now," he said, "but they used to be giants. A wizard turned them into windmills to protect them from my attack."

Poor Sancho shrugged and helped Don Quixote back onto his horse. When would Don Quixote ever learn!

*Don Quixote aimed his lance right at the sail of the windmill. Just then a puff of wind turned the sail and Don Quixote was knocked off his horse.*

# HUCK TEARS UP HIS LETTER

Huckleberry Finn was confused.

For weeks he had been traveling down the Mississippi River on a raft after running away from home. Huck's father was notorious in Hannibal, Missouri for drinking too much and for mistreating his son. Finally Huck had escaped from the cabin where his father had kept him locked up.

Before he had gone to live with his father, Huck had lived with Miss Watson, an elderly woman who owned a slave named Jim. One night Jim overheard a slave dealer offer to buy him from Miss Watson. Afraid he would be sold far away from his family, Jim hid on a nearby island — the same one where Huck was hiding from his father. Jim and Huck decided to travel together to safety.

For weeks they had many adventures on the river. Once Huck dressed up as a girl and went to a farmhouse to see if he could hear any news from home. Another time Huck put a dead snake in Jim's blanket hoping to scare him. Instead, Jim was bitten and almost died when a live snake curled up next to the dead one. After he played that trick, Huck decided not to be mean to Jim anymore.

One night a large riverboat ran over the raft and Jim and Huck had to dive deep into the water to avoid being hit by the paddlewheel. They swam to opposite sides of the river and for several weeks thought each other dead.

Now Huck was struggling to know what to do. Jim had been captured by a family that suspected he was a runaway slave. They wanted his owner to give them a reward but they didn't know who Miss Watson was or where she lived. But Huck knew.

Huck also knew that everyone would expect him to help Miss Watson get her slave back because people in those days thought slaves were property that could be bought and sold.

Huck wasn't so sure. Still, he wrote a letter to Miss Watson telling her where she could find Jim.

And then Huck started thinking. He remembered all the times he had heard Jim crying for his children. Huck remembered the many nights when Jim let him sleep instead of waking him up to take his turn watching out for the raft.

Huck knew Jim wasn't just someone's property but was a living human being with real feelings. More than that, Jim was Huck's friend.

With a sudden rip, Huck tore up the letter he had written. Even if everyone thought he was wrong, he would help Jim get to freedom instead.

*Huck knew Jim wasn't just someone's property but was a living human being with real feelings. More than that, Jim was Huck's friend.*

# THE BISHOP AND JEAN VALJEAN

A cold wind was blowing when Jean Valjean opened the heavy door of the inn and ducked inside. "I want a room for the night," he told the innkeeper. "Certainly, sir," the innkeeper said, handing Jean the registration book. "Sign your name and show your identification."

Jean felt his face turning hot with embarrassment. He pulled a yellow paper from his wallet and handed it to the innkeeper.

"This paper says you are a criminal!" the innkeeper said.

"I just got out of prison," Jean explained. "Many years ago I stole a loaf of bread to feed my sister's children. They were starving!"

The innkeeper grabbed the registration book from Jean. "Go away!" he said.

"But I served my time!" Jean said. "I was in jail for nineteen years! Surely I have paid my debt for one loaf of bread!"

But the innkeeper would not let him stay. Nor would the next innkeeper, nor the next. That night Jean slept outside in the cold under a pile of trash.

The next day Jean was desperately cold and hungry. He knocked on the door of a church and was surprised to find himself welcomed inside.

"I'm a convict," Jean explained, but Bishop Myriel was a kind man who gave him a warm dinner and a soft bed.

Still, Jean didn't trust him. That night while the Bishop slept, Jean stole some of his silverware and ran away.

Several policemen saw him running and stopped him. When they searched Jean's bag, they recognized the silverware.

"Once a thief, always a thief," one of the policemen said, but just then Bishop Myriel came hurrying up the street.

"Dear sir!" he called to Jean. "You left in such a hurry you forgot to take the candlesticks I gave you, too."

Jean knew that the Bishop had not given him the candlesticks. What was he trying to do? The policemen didn't know what to think either.

"Well," they said, "we can't arrest you if the Bishop gave you these things. You are free to go."

After the policemen left Jean went with the Bishop back to his home. He listened as Bishop Myriel spoke.

"I believe you can be a good man if you want to," he said. "Take this silver and use it to become an honest man. It is a gift from me to help you start your new life as someone who helps other people."

Jean was so moved by this act of forgiveness that he did as Bishop Myriel said, living the rest of his life in service to others.

*"I believe you can be a good man if you want to," said Bishop Myriel. "Take this silver and use it to become an honest man. It is a gift from me to help you start your new life."*

# GLOSSARY OF VIRTUES

**Compassion**

Literally, to "suffer with." To take pity.

*Brother Martin had compassion on the poor, even giving up his own bed to a beggar.*

**Confidence**

Believing in yourself. Self-assurance.

*The bookseller was confident he would find his treasure, even when others laughed.*

**Empathy**

Putting yourself in another's shoes. Understanding how others feel.

*Young Prince Cherry lacked empathy, caring for no one but himself.*

**Faith**

To trust what another tells you. To believe.

*Growing up blind and deaf trapped Helen Keller in her own world, but Helen's parents had faith that Annie Sullivan would free her.*

**Foresight**

Wise planning for the future.

*Odysseus's foresight in having his men hide among the sheep enabled them to escape the Cyclops.*

**Forgiveness**

Pardoning someone who has harmed you.

*Bishop Myriel forgave Jean Valjean for stealing his silverware.*

**Hope**

To desire something and believe you'll achieve it.

*Frederick Douglass never gave up hope he would learn to read.*

**Judgement**

To make good decisions. To choose wisely.

*Don Quixote showed bravery but poor judgement when he charged the windmills.*

**Leadership**

Being the first to take a position or make a decision — especially when it's difficult or dangerous.

*The Banyan Deer was a true leader when he went to face the Sultan and hunters himself.*

**Loyalty**

Being true to a person or group.

*Huck was loyal to Jim when he refused to turn Jim in as a runaway slave.*

**Perseverance**

Not giving up in achieving a project or goal.

*Yu persevered in calling for help for his brother Nikki Tikki Tumbo.*

**Sacrifice**

To give up some good thing for a higher purpose.

*Rainbow Crow sacrificed his beautiful feathers and singing voice to bring fire to the animals.*

**Sharing**

Letting others use your possessions.

*Little Peachling shared his dumplings with his friends as he set out for the ogres' castle.*

**Sportsmanship**

Competing vigorously, fairly and courteously.

*When Roland and Oliver fought, they awed the crowd with their sportsmanship.*